To

_____

from

_____

May this little book inspire you
to live in joy, peace, and Light.

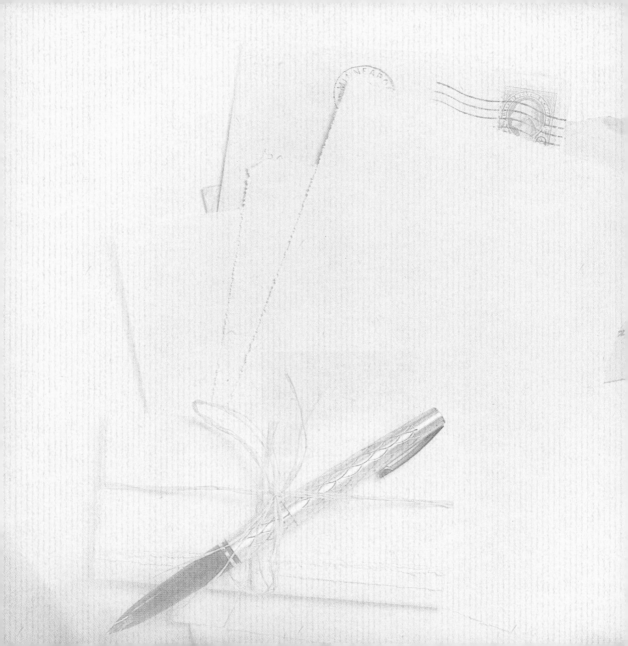

Touched by the
LIGHT

*Inspirational Reflections
from the Artist and His Friends*

THOMAS KINKADE

With Robert C. Larson

COUNTRYMAN

Copyright © 2003 by Thomas Kinkade, Media Arts Group, Inc.,
Morgan Hill, California

Published by J. Countryman®, a division of Thomas Nelson, Inc.,
Nashville, Tennessee 37214

J. Countryman® is a trademark of Thomas Nelson, Inc.

Unless otherwise indicated, all Scripture quotations in this book are
from the New King James Version (NKJV) © 1979, 1980, 1982, 1992.
Thomas Nelson, Inc. publisher.

Design: Koechel Peterson & Associates, Inc., Minneapolis, Minnesota

Project Editor: Kathy Baker

ISBN 1 4041 0012 1

Printed and bound in Belgium

www.thomasnelson.com

www.jcountryman.com

www.thomaskinkade.com

Table of Contents

And God said, "Let there be light," and there was light.

For God, such an act was undoubtedly a snap. That's the business of *divine fiat*. Speak it—and it is accomplished. Simple for God; not so easy for an artist's who's spent his entire life with a heart open to receiving that divine light, after which he mixes a few daubs of paint, takes out some sticks with hair on them, and splashes his inspiration on tiny bits of cloth. No *divine fiat* here. Just hard work, sitting before a canvas with a heart moved to deliver the message that almighty God is the original Painter of light, and that His Son, Jesus Christ, is the Light for our world of shadows and darkness.

And that is the purpose of this book, *Touched by the Light*—to honor the One who brings lasting light into our lives. That's why the following pages are not about Thomas Kinkade and his accomplishments as a painter. Instead, what follows is about the Light of God that this artist sees continually emerging from distant hills, roaring seas, placid streams, quiet gardens, and dazzling skies that represent every color of the spectrum.

The book is also a testimony to how this God—ordained luminance, when transferred to canvas, has somehow touched people's emotions in ways this painter never could have dreamed possible—something for which I am grateful beyond words.

Touched by the Light is a prayer that God will move your spirit and touch your heart with both the selected paintings and the words that follow—especially the words of Scripture that speak to the majesty of God and the richness of a creation that He gave us to enjoy.

Right now a merciful, light—filled, heavenly Father wants you to trust His love, compassion, power, and beauty. He wants you to know that the radiance He offers is all the light you will ever need to sustain your faith and to live as His faithful servant in a darkened world.

The choice is yours and the choice is mine—and it really is very simple, not dissimilar to using the on/off switch on the wall. You and I have the option to choose either light or darkness; joy or despair; a meditative heart bathed in the dazzling light of God's Son, or the crazy, unredemptive cacophony of a media—saturated world gone mad.

*It's my prayer
that you will choose
God's light today,
and for all the todays
yet to come.*

THOMAS KINKADE
CARMEL, CALIFORNIA
APRIL 2003

The LORD is my shepherd;

I shall not want.

He makes me to lie down in green pastures;

He leads me...

Beside Still Waters

They're often referred to as the most comforting verses in all of Holy Scripture . . .

The LORD is my shepherd; I shall not want. He makes me to lie down in green pastures;
He leads me beside the still waters.

God's words of peace and serenity. No raging torrents here, no angry current cascading over sharp granite, spilling into swift–moving, rock–strewn steams far below. Not in Psalm 23. Here are only words of assurance, calm, peace, and consolation as we are invited to come alongside *still waters*—my inspiration for this painting.

As I sat in front of my easel and made my heart quiet before God, I prayed that He would direct my brushstrokes so they'd touch a heart with how Eden might have appeared to earth's first couple. Pristine. Warm. Hopeful. Inviting. I wanted this remote hideaway, bathed in silvery light, to blaze with flowers of every hue and description, silent save for the murmur of gently rushing waters.

Each time I approach these quiet waters, I bow to the mystery and wonder of God's creation during those eons long ago when nature was perfect. Unspoiled. An instant in time when there was neither pollution of the heart nor a noxious physical environment. It was a moment when waters were pure. Still. Soul–quenching waters that later would assuage thirsty hearts and bring hope to drought–prone spirits, providing lasting refreshment and spiritual nourishment, which only a relationship with the living God could provide.

The good news is that these *still waters* remain, although too often sequestered in the out–of–the–way places of life, waiting for you and me to discover their quiet power. If our hearts are open to the de*lightful* message of the Savior, we will indeed find those bountiful, refreshing streams that satisfy—living water, which gives us lasting sustenance and a reason to live. Distractions be gone! Beginning now, may we come into God's quiet presence as we celebrate the joy of being touched by the gentle waters of light and life.

Mr. Kinkade,

A Friend . . . *Touched by the Light*

Your paintings bring back a tender memory I had with my dad on Mother's Day, 1987. I was not a Christian at the time, so I did not truly understand what my dad had said. My father had leukemia and was dying. He had been in a coma all of Mother's Day. Later in the day, when my mom and both of my brothers were together in his room, he came out of his coma. We were all blessed with the opportunity to talk with him one last time and say important things such as, "I love you."

I remember the excited look in his eyes as he kept repeating, "I want to celebrate." To me this was crazy. He was dying. Why would he want to celebrate? I asked him why, and he said he'd spoken with the Lord, and that He had a place waiting for him . . . and it was beautiful.

Although I didn't understand it at the time, a seed was planted and God became a reality to me. Years later, I gave my heart to the Lord. One day I entered one of your galleries, and I felt as though your paintings portrayed a taste of heaven. The Lord has truly blessed you, and God's love shows in your paintings . . . especially *Beside Still Waters*. Your works are a reminder that good things lie ahead, and that my dad is in a beautiful place with the Lord.

SUE FAUS

TOUCHED BY THE
LIGHT OF GOD'S WORD

The statutes of the LORD are right, rejoicing the heart;
The commandment of the LORD is pure, enlightening the eyes;
The fear of the LORD is clean, enduring forever;
The judgments of the LORD are true and righteous altogether.

PSALM 19:8–9

The LORD is my shepherd; I shall not want.

He makes me to lie down in green pastures;

He leads me beside the still waters.

He restores my soul;

He leads me in the paths of righteousness

For His name's sake.

Yea, though I walk through the valley

of the shadow of death,

I will fear no evil; For You are with me;

Your rod and Your staff, they comfort me.

You prepare a table before me in the presence

of my enemies; You anoint my head

with oil; My cup runs over.

Surely goodness and mercy shall follow me

All the days of my life;

And I will dwell in the house of the LORD

Forever.

PSALM 23

Touched by the Light of Experience

*I think most of us look at personal delights as somewhere
between minimally important and borderline immoral. We like them,
but we're not sure we ought to. We seldom give them the high priority
when other demands are competing for our attention. Nevertheless,
the soul feeds on simple joys and withers without them.*

VICTORIA MORAN

A Prayer to the Giver of Light

Dear Father in heaven, when the storms
of life surround us, and when the clatter and
disturbance of living cause us to take our eyes
off of You, direct us to those still, quiet waters,
where we come into Your presence as children
in need of Your quiet, gentle touch. Help us
to focus on You, love You, and learn more of
You and Your beloved Son. As we are filled
with Your presence, we know You promise to
prepare our own hearts to become purveyors
of light to all who come to us for comfort.
Amen.

Lord my God,
give me a mind to know you,
a heart to seek you,
wisdom to find you, and . . .
a hope of finally embracing you.

THOMAS AQUINAS

Your mercy, O LORD, is in the heavens;

Your faithfulness reaches to the clouds.

Your righteousness is like the

great mountains...

PSALM 36:5-6

Yosemite Valley

Welcome to one of the most magnificent examples of God's majesty on the face of the earth—Yosemite Valley. This painting attempts to depict the mighty work of the Creator's hand as seen from a little-known place called *Artist's Point*, named in tribute to the many nineteenth-century artists who favored this location as a sketching ground.

I'll never forget my first visit to Yosemite Valley as a young artist. I was overwhelmed, awestruck, virtually immobilized by the power and grandeur of the largest piece of exposed granite on earth. I never fully recovered from the experience!

As I stood there, my faith was strengthened. My heart filled with joy, and I sensed the presence of God course through my being. As I reflected on my life and work on subsequent trips to the Yosemite Valley, I always knew God would continue to put me, my easel, paints, canvases and brushes in perspective. For how could I even come close to doing justice to what God had created? That's when I found myself echoing the words from Psalm 8:4

. . . what is man that You are mindful of him?

Yosemite Valley possesses a clarity of light not observable in many places on this earth—light that spills off the vastness of sheer cliffs and shrouds the cloudy sky at sunset. Again and again, I have been touched by its light—the light of nature, but, more important, the light of our heavenly Father who created such a masterpiece for us to enjoy.

And here's where I want to give you a word of encouragement: You, too, are an artist of the Light, whether you are a painter or not. That's because you have the God–given opportunities to paint light for others with your tender acts of kindness, your gestures of humility, and your words of comfort and cheer.

Together let us celebrate our mutual gifts as painters of God's light as we extend ourselves to help those who live in darkness.

A Friend...Touched by the Light

No matter how dark our life at times may seem, the Lord always lets the light of hope and serenity shine through. It was during this dark time that I first discovered your work—and it helped me immeasurably. Seeing the light of the Lord shining through your paintings helped me to give myself and my problems to Him. In the process, He showed me the way to peace and serenity I had longed for. Because of these dark days in my life, my love of the Lord and commitment to Him are stronger than ever.

JOANNE MARCHETTI QUINN

TOUCHED BY THE LIGHT
OF GOD'S WORD

By awesome deeds in righteousness

    You will answer us,

O God of our salvation,

You who are the confidence of all the ends

    of the earth,

And of the far–off seas;

Who established the mountains by His strength,

Being clothed with power;

You who still the noise of the seas,

The noise of their waves,

And the tumult of the peoples.

PSALM 65:5–7

Your mercy, O LORD, is in the heavens;
Your faithfulness reaches to the clouds.
Your righteousness is like the great mountains;
Your judgments are a great deep;
O LORD, You preserve man and beast.
How precious is Your lovingkindness, O God!
Therefore the children of men put their trust under
the shadow of Your wings.

PSALM 36: 5–7

Touched by the Light of Experience

God will not compel the adoration of men: it would be but pagan worship that would bring to His altars.

He will rouse in men a sense of need, which shall grow at length into a longing; He will make them feel after Him,

until by their search becoming able to behold Him, He may at length reveal to them the glory of their Father.

He works silently—keeps quiet behind His works, as it were, that He may truly reveal Himself in the right time.

GEORGE MACDONALD; FLEMING H. REVEL

A Prayer to the Giver of Light

Gracious God, thank You for the majesty and power that You display in Your mighty acts of creation: the mountains, seas, forests, sunrises, and sunsets. Too often I take Your magnificence for granted, perhaps because my eyes remain too dim to see the whole; too distracted to see the fullness of Your light. Lord, remove the scales from my eyes that I may see You and Your creation with renewed vision. Thank You for reminding me that You are God and that I am not. Lord, as of this moment, I step back and immerse myself in the presence of Your power. I am silent. I relinquish all control of my life to You. My deepest prayer is that You will craft me into the person You designed me to be. Thank You for painting Your light into my life.

You will keep him in perfect peace

Whose mind is stayed on You,

Because he trusts in You.

ISAIAH 26:3

The End of a
Perfect Day

Thomas Kinkade

Paintings such as *End of a Perfect Day* express my growing admiration for the serenity and beauty of nature untamed. The rustic stone cabin is a secluded jewel, nestled in a setting where most of us would like to live; the light on the distant snowcapped mountains speaks of a power and grandeur that all the world's gizmos and gadgets will never reproduce. At the end of every day—perfect or not—my prayer always remains: *The LORD is my light and my salvation; whom shall I fear?* (Psalm 27:1)

However, in our world of blaring TV sets, obsession with checking our email, and the nonstop necessity to possess endless streams of stuff, I think most of us would agree that increased production ultimately leads to decreased meaning and a darkness of the human spirit. I sense that we've lost our need to be touched by the light. Technology can be a lifesaver; it can also be a life killer. Which is more beneficial to the human spirit? To sit quietly in the shade at the end of the day and be struck with awe at God's handiwork, or to stare at a screen and mindlessly watch sitcoms? I think these are important questions.

You and I do need not be isolationists from the rest of life, but we do have the option to place ourselves in settings that nourish our souls and fill our hearts with sustenance. It's my prayer as you read these words, explore these paintings, and immerse yourself in the reflections of my friends, that you will make a personal commitment to be touched by God's light, slow your pace, celebrate the beauty of our heavenly Father's creation, and begin to see the beginning and end of every day in ways you've never experienced them before.

A Friend . . . Touched by the Light

I bought two small prints of yours in the last two months,

one of which is *End of a Perfect Day*. I'm enjoying your works

so very much because they show

your family values, and how you

put God first in all you do. God has blessed you so much, and,

in return, you have lifted Him up in all your paintings. I can just

feel the love of God in your work.

A few years ago the Lord took my husband home to Glory at

the age of 54. But God fills up the holes and hurts, and has left

me with more love than I'll ever know. I am one who also

loves the Lord Jesus Christ, and I sense that same spirit in your

paintings. I just wanted you to know how I feel.

BETTY J. MULLEN

God fills up the holes and hurts, and has left me with more love

TOUCHED BY THE
LIGHT OF GOD'S WORD

The LORD is my light and my salvation;

Whom shall I fear?

The LORD is the strength of my life;

Of whom shall I be afraid?

When the wicked came against me

To eat up my flesh,

My enemies and foes,

They stumbled and fell.

Though an army may encamp against me,

My heart shall not fear;

Though war may rise against me,

In this I will be confident.

PSALM 27:1–3

They are abundantly satisfied with the fullness of Your house,

And You give them drink from the river of Your pleasures.

For with You is the fountain of life;

In Your light we see light.

Oh, continue Your lovingkindness to those who know You,

And Your righteousness to the upright in heart.

PSALM 36:8–10

Touched by the Light of Experience

We need to find God, and He cannot be
found in noise and restlessness. God is the
friend of silence. See how nature—trees,
flowers, grass—grow in silence; see the stars,
the moon and the sun, how they move in
silence . . . the more we receive in silent
prayer, the more we can give in our active
life. We need silence to be able to touch souls.
The essential thing is not what we say,
but what God says to us and through us.

MOTHER TERESA

Have courage
for the great sorrows of life
and have the patience for the small ones;
and when you have laboriously
achieved your daily task,
go to sleep in peace. God is awake.

VICTOR HUGO

A Prayer to the Giver of Light

Father, thank You for giving us Your perfect ending to every day. Whether we've been faithful to You or not; whether we've been the kind of person You created us to be or not, we can still thank You for bringing our each day to a close with Your abundant forgiveness, love, and understanding. We also thank You for the heavenly light You continually shine on our paths—a brightness from above that keeps us from stumbling and from falling off cliffs. You, the original and only true painter of light, use Your divine brushstrokes to give us glorious sunsets, quiet streams, majestic mountains, and clouds of every color and hue—a natural world that can only declare Your majesty. May we, as Your humble servants, each day be as faithful in our praise of You and Your Son as is the handiwork of Your creation. Thank You, Father, for removing the darkness from our lives and for leaving us rich in spirit with Your holy light. Amen.

You will bring them in and plant them

In the mountain of Your inheritance,

In the place, O LORD, which You have made

For Your own dwelling,

The sanctuary, O LORD, which Your hands

have established.

EXODUS 15:17

The Mountain Chapel

Long before the great architects and designers of history created enormous cathedrals and places of worship, God graced us with natural sanctuaries, painted with the radiant light of His divine love and peace. In *The Mountain Chapel* I have sought to capture this presence of a living God in the stream, forests, mountains and valleys—all of which He has given us to enjoy. Situated among the tranquility of these natural settings stands another beacon of comfort and hope—a friendly, quiet, lighted chapel—one more symbol that exists to glorify and praise our heavenly Father.

When we think of worshipping God, our minds often retreat to confined, enclosed spaces: a building, wooden pews, elevated altar, and an array of stained glass. Although we are not to avoid assembling with others in such an environment, we also can be with God in less-structured places. For my work, I routinely travel to quiet places of nature where I see God's majesty in the great textures, creative shapes, and combinations of colors and forms. My sketchpad is seldom far from me, because I never know when God will touch me in an extraordinary way with the beauty of His hand.

I hope you feel that same sense of God's presence as you allow nature to speak to you in your own life. May the mountains, the valleys, the streams, and the many forms of sky all around you capture your heart in fresh, new ways. Let them wash over you as a cleansing. As you do, keep your eyes on the Creator, the source of all light, joy, and blessing, who gives to you from His bountiful, creative heart. Find your own mountain chapel; live in quiet peace as often as you can—away from the noise of the world and its cares.

A Friend . . . Touched by the Light

When we gaze at your paintings,
a deep sense of peace and tranquility
comes over us. The doctors cannot
explain why my husband is beating the
odds in his battle against cancer.
However, we truly believe it is largely
due to our positive mental attitude, our
love of sharing, and our outlook on life.

The state of mind that your paintings
put into us, and the stress relief your
work provides, have contributed, we
believe, to our successful battle against
this evil. Thank you for all you have
done for us, and for the world,
by providing us with the opportunity
to experience your works of art.

Peace, love, and healing.

DEBRA D. SAMUEL

TOUCHED BY THE
LIGHT OF GOD'S WORD

The people who walked in darkness
Have seen a great light;
Those who dwelt in the land of the shadow of death,
Upon them a light has shined.
You have multiplied the nation
And increased its joy;
They rejoice before You
According to the joy of harvest . . .

ISAIAH 9:2–3

Then I turned myself to consider wisdom

and madness and folly;

For what can the man do who succeeds the king?—

Only what he has already done.

Then I saw that wisdom excels folly

As light excels darkness.

The wise man's eyes are in his head,

But the fool walks in darkness.

Yet I myself perceived

That the same event happens to them all.

ECCLESIASTES 2:12–14

Touched by the Light of Experience

Give light, and the darkness will disappear of itself.

DESIDERIUS ERASMUS

When it is dark enough,
you can see the stars.

CHARLES A. BEARD

Darkness is my point of view,
my right to myself; light
is God's point of view.

OSWALD CHAMBERS

A Prayer to the Giver of Light

Eternal Father, You dwell so high above us that we cannot fully understand You, and yet You are so much a part of us that we cannot remove ourselves from You. Thank You for thinking of us when You created a world of such beauty and splendor. We are sorry that we've sullied it with trash, polluted it with our excess, and brought into it the clatter of a manmade world, all of which flies in the face of Your grandeur. Teach us to respect Your creation and to experience Your holy presence in both the ravages and serenity of nature. Give us a new platform for praise. Help us to celebrate Your goodness, and prepare our hearts to worship You both within the cathedral and without. Take away our limiting boundaries, expand our awareness, and grant us the true freedom that can only come through a relationship with Your Son. These things we ask, because You are our Father, our Creator, our hope for today, and for all days yet to come. Amen.

He stirs up the sea with His power,

And by His understanding He breaks up the storm.

JOB 26:4

Conquering the Storms

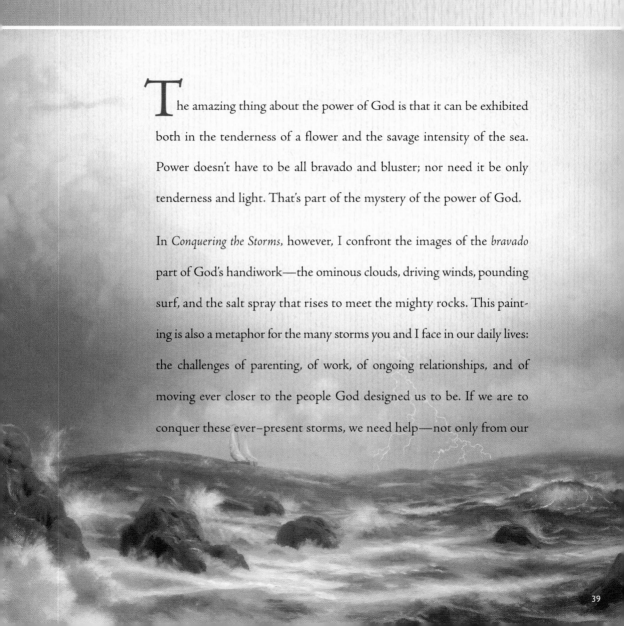

The amazing thing about the power of God is that it can be exhibited both in the tenderness of a flower and the savage intensity of the sea. Power doesn't have to be all bravado and bluster; nor need it be only tenderness and light. That's part of the mystery of the power of God.

In *Conquering the Storms*, however, I confront the images of the *bravado* part of God's handiwork—the ominous clouds, driving winds, pounding surf, and the salt spray that rises to meet the mighty rocks. This painting is also a metaphor for the many storms you and I face in our daily lives: the challenges of parenting, of work, of ongoing relationships, and of moving ever closer to the people God designed us to be. If we are to conquer these ever–present storms, we need help—not only from our friends, but also from the light of divine intervention that will never leave us or forsake us.

That's why there is light in the lighthouse in this painting. For ships, the light is a beacon of protection; for one seeking the safe harbor of God's truth, it depicts a vertical relationship with Jesus Christ, the Light of the world.

We need to be continually reminded that there's not enough obscurity in the universe to extinguish the light of a single candle. Neither is there enough darkness to quench the human spirit—not as long as we allow God to *keep our own light burning brightly*: a light of hope, love, and encouragement. Just as the person of Jesus Christ is the Light of the world, so are we to be light in a world of shadows and despair. It's my prayer for you that your light will always shine, and that, with God's help, you will be able to conquer any storm.

God Kept conquering those

storms for me

A Friend...Touched by the Light

During the past few years, my dream was to own one of your paintings so I could see the light up close and personal. Recently, I finally was able to purchase *Conquering the Storms*. This is a work of art that is very personal to me. In my life, since I was small, I have ridden in a boat that faced almost continual storms. But God kept conquering those storms for me, all of which made me stronger...

I want you to know you are an inspiration to me, especially on those days when I just hang on with the tips of my fingers. Your painting is in my bedroom, where I see it the last moment before sleep and when I awake. You are a blessing. Thank you.

JULIET ANN HIRSCHY

TOUCHED BY THE
LIGHT OF GOD'S WORD

Then they cry out to the LORD

in their trouble,

And He brings them out of

their distresses.

He calms the storm,

So that its waves are still.

Then they are glad because

they are quiet;

So He guides them to their

desired haven.

PSALM 107:28–30

All things were made through Him,
and without Him nothing was made
that was made. In Him was life, and the
life was the light of men. And the light shines
in the darkness, and the darkness did not
comprehend it.

JOHN 1:3–5

Inspiration without
perspiration leads to
frustration and stagnation.

BILL BRIGHT

Touched by the Light of Experience

The clouds of concern may completely circle us today,
but God will remove them in His own good time and will provide
direction for us if we simply trust Him and wait upon Him.

WOODROW KROLL

It was among the Parthians
the custom that none were to give
their children any meat in the
morning before they saw the sweat
on their faces . . . You shall find this
to be God's usual course:
not to give His children the taste
of His delights until they begin
to sweat in seeking after Him.

RICHARD BAXTER

A Prayer to the Giver of Light

Our heavenly Father, give us the hope
to keep living amid the hurt, pain, and
storms of life. Keep us singing in the
darkness, with the secure knowledge that
You are a good Father, who wants only
the best for His children. Give us the
light of Jesus Christ to illuminate our
path, so that we may walk with integrity
according to the divine plan. Keep hope
alive in our hearts always, as we trust You
in both the light and dark places: when
the sun rises in all its brilliance and
while we struggle to keep our small boats
afloat in the storms at sea. Help us to
know there is land ahead, a lighthouse
of safety, and a welcoming harbor. May
we always remember that You are holding
our hands. Thank You for the satisfaction
that can only be found in You, the One
who paints the light of life that gives
direction for our lives. Amen.

My people will dwell in a peaceful habitation,

In secure dwellings, and in quiet resting places.

ISAIAH 32:18

A Quiet Evening

The image of a stream and the hush of its slowly moving waters; a cottage that welcomes a weary traveler; inviting plumes of smoke that rise from its chimneys; light from windows that speak only of peace and acceptance. The heart has its special places, quiet retreats, fragrant with the sweet perfume of flowers, bathed in the romantic light of sunset. This is one of the most tranquil scenes I've ever painted, and it is one to which I often return when life, for me, becomes a swirl of self–imposed turmoil.

You and I were not designed to breathe in the fetid air of five o'clock traffic. Nor do I think God had banal television programs, media hype, worthless purchases, and soul pollution in mind when He created the universe, giving special attention to the planet on which we live. So what do we do? Settle for the worst? Accept the mentality of the herd? Or, do we make the time to search out that quiet evening of the soul and go there to find respite for our weary hearts?

Just as there is a softness to the edges of this painting, so must there be a softness at the extremities of our lives—a gentleness that shows itself in kindness to others, that displays an open mind and free spirit, that speaks encouraging words to those who have lost all hope, providing help to friends who've lost their way. This is best done when the heart is at rest. Quiet. Attentive to the living God and to the message of peace spoken and lived by His Son Jesus Christ.

A quiet evening . . .

a time of peace . . .

a life worth living . . .

a time to *be still*,

and know that I am God.

PSALM 46:10

A Friend...Touched by the Light

I want to thank you for using your God-given talents, and for developing them in such a way as to bring love, peace, and joy to others. Thank you for making the world a happier place for people like me. I wish you and your family much happiness and joy for many years to come!

MARY E. NELSON

You and your family must feel great pride when your friends tell you about the love they see in your artistic talents. We are all here for a purpose, and you certainly have found yours. May you and your lovely family have happy, healthy lives, with thanks from one of your very happy patrons.

DELORES Y. HENDRICKS

TOUCHED BY THE LIGHT
OF GOD'S WORD

Pray for the peace of Jerusalem:

"May they prosper who love you.

Peace be within your walls,

Prosperity within your palaces."

For the sake of my brethren and companions,

I will now say, "Peace be within you."

PSALM 122:6–8

It shall come to pass in that day

That there will be no light;

The lights will diminish.

It shall be one day

Which is known to the LORD—

Neither day nor night.

But at evening time it shall happen

That it will be light.

ZECHARIAH 14:6–7

Touched by the Light of Experience

But whenever you do come upon this silence, it seems as though you have received a gift, one which is "promising" in the true sense of the word. The promise of this silence is that new life can be born. It is this silence which is the silence of peace and prayer, because you are brought back to the other who is leading you. In this silence you lose the feeling of being compulsive and you find yourself a person who can be himself along with other things and other people.

HENRI J. M. NOUWEN

A Prayer to the Giver of Light

Dear Lord, give us an attitude of quiet peace as we meet the challenges of *now*. While we look with anticipation to the future, let not our obsession for tomorrow remove our passion for today. Only You know what will confront us at the next bend of road. We have only the moment at hand to do Your bidding. Grant us the wisdom to live this day in quietness, peace, and love as we do our best to distance ourselves from the distractions that confuse us. Help us find our own quiet evening of the spirit, where we can retreat to find solace and comfort. Remove the noise of life that dims our view of You and Your creation. Eradicate that which stirs our anxiety and keeps us trapped in a world not of Your design. May the beauty of Your universe surround us, the comfort of Your peace engulf us, and the joy of serving You make us whole. Remove the sharpened edges of our lives, and grant us the softness of Your divine light. In Your name we pray, Amen.

Thomas
Kinkade

The work of righteousness
will be peace,
And the effect of righteousness,
quietness and assurance forever.

ISAIAH 32:17

If we care anything about Christ at all,
our hearts will turn to Him as naturally as,
when the winter begins to pinch, the migrating
birds seek the sunny south, turning by an instinct
that they do not themselves understand.

ALEXANDER MACLAREN

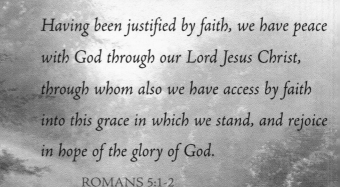

Having been justified by faith, we have peace with God through our Lord Jesus Christ, through whom also we have access by faith into this grace in which we stand, and rejoice in hope of the glory of God.

ROMANS 5:1-2

Stairway to Paradise

Thomas Kinkade

The only true stairway to paradise comes from a life that pleases the living God and moves through its days conformed to the image of His Son Jesus Christ. Yet, multitudes travel all manner of life's *other* staircases in hopes of discovering their true selves. Some climb hastily, with little regard for others, in their attempted ascents to fame and fortune. Others are more methodical in their quests, convinced that self–discovery lies at the other end of the staircase, and that, they hope, a guru in white robes awaits their arrival, complete with high–sounding counsel that promises to unveil the mysteries of life. The less–patient climbers forego the staircase altogether and look for the nearest escalator to take them to the top.

The writer of Proverbs describes various ways people try to get to the top of the stairs:

> By pride comes nothing but strife,
> But with the well–advised is wisdom.
> Wealth gained by dishonesty will be diminished,
> But he who gathers by labor will increase.
> Hope deferred makes the heart sick,
> But when the desire comes, it is a tree of life.
>
> PROVERBS 13:10–12

In this painting, the small dabs of light punctuating the stairway are symbolic of what keeps us moving in an upward direction. God never gives us all the light *we think we need* at one time. But He always gives enough light, enough truth, and enough insight for the challenges at hand. Our job is simply to keep climbing the staircase, to take one step at a time, and to use the light of His divine presence to guide our trek upward. We cannot know what lies beyond the last visible step. We can be certain, however, that our heavenly Father will not coax us to the top of the stairs only to drop us into a darkened abyss. He's not that kind of Father. He will neither leave us nor forsake us.

I encourage you to stop and gaze at this painting. Reflect on your own life's journey. Then, let's join hands, begin to walk the stairs together, and climb ever closer toward that eternal light that awaits God's children.

A Friend...Touched by the Light

You may never be able to fully understand or comprehend on this earth how much your paintings affect people. I found "my" painting, *Stairway to Paradise,* at the lowest point of my life.

I had just buried my mother after her ten long months of battling lung cancer. After mom died, I was at the Mall of Georgia just looking around when I saw the gallery. After a while, I saw *Stairway to Paradise.* As I stood there looking at the flowers, the climbing roses and, of course, the light, my first thought was that Mom would love this garden. By this time, I couldn't see the painting anymore because of the tears. Being embarrassed about crying in public, I left the gallery.

But I couldn't stay away long. Every time I went to the mall—any mall—I had to go and find "my" painting. Each time, I would sit on the sofa in the viewing room and just cry. This became a regular Sunday afternoon event for me, and each time I would discover something different about the painting. Eventually, my husband purchased the painting and gave it to me for my birthday. It's a prayer of mine that someday, this side of heaven, the Lord will allow me to meet you face to face, so I can thank you, in person, for painting *Stairway to Paradise* just for me! Your sister in Christ.

LARAE FLOWERS

TOUCHED BY THE LIGHT
OF GOD'S WORD

By the Fountain Gate, in front of them, they went up
the stairs of the City of David, on the stairway
of the wall, beyond the house of David . . .

NEHEMIAH 12:37

The earth is the LORD's, and all its fullness,

The world and those who dwell therein.

For He has founded it upon the seas,

And established it upon the waters.

Who may ascend into the hill of the LORD?

Or who may stand in His holy place?

He who has clean hands and a pure heart,

Who has not lifted up his soul to an idol,

Nor sworn deceitfully.

He shall receive blessing from the LORD,

And righteousness from the God

of his salvation.

PSALM 24:1–5

*Aim at heaven,
and you will get earth
thrown in; aim at earth,
and you will get neither.*

C. S. LEWIS

Touched by the Light of Experience

*Lord, give me faith!—to live from day to day,
With tranquil heart to do my simple part,
And, with my hand in Thine, just go Thy way.*

*Lord, give me faith!—to trust, if not to know;
With quiet mind in all things Thee to find,
And, child—like, to go where Thou wouldst have me go.*

*Lord, give me faith!—to leave it all to Thee,
The future is Thy gift, I would not lift
The Veil Thy love has hung 'twixt it and me.*

JOHN OXENHAM

A Prayer to the Giver of Light

Lord, give us the courage to climb the staircase. Help us to know we are not alone in our ascent, but that You are with us always to guide our most tentative steps. Give us faith—mighty faith. Give us strength—mighty strength. Give us the courage to keep on climbing, with the profound knowledge that You know what lies beyond. May we believe with Martin Luther that faith is a living, daring confidence in Your grace, so sure and certain that one could stake his life on it a thousand times. Dear God, let that be our earnest prayer as we climb our own stairways to paradise and into the arms of the Eternal. Make us dead to doubts, dumb to discouragements, and blind to impossibilities. Keep the light of Your countenance burning brightly, so that on our journey upward we may neither falter nor slip. We thank You in advance for answering our prayer. Amen.

LORD, I have loved the habitation of Your hot

And the place where Your glory dwells.

PSALM 26:8

Home is Where

the Heart Is

Thomas
Kinkade

Without a consciousness of darkness, there can be little or no awareness of light. Friends often ask me how I go about painting light. It often surprises them when I say that I start with massive amounts of darkness, applying glaze upon glaze that cast great shadows of dark on the canvases. Only after those pieces of cloth are saturated with darkness do I allow the light to emerge—and often only small pools of light at that.

In *Home is Where the Heart Is* I tap into much of the darkness of my own life—those deep, frightening shadows that broke my family apart when I was only five years old. Now much older and, I hope, wiser, I'm certain that without that darkness of separation and abandonment—that glaze piled upon human glaze of disappointment and despair—I would not be able to comprehend what a real home looks like.

Idealistic? Unrealistic in today's divorce-prone world? Fantasy thinking? Hardly. The home does not need to be an idyllic cottage ringed with fragrant flowers and cobbled path leading to the front door. Nor must it have a wicker chair on the porch that invites friends and strangers to stop and rest. The teddy bear beneath the tree and the swing? Both optional.

What is *mandatory*, however, is that the home be a place of love, harmony, peace, and acceptance. To turn the phrase, *the heart is also where the home is*—be it a one-room walk-up, efficiency apartment, condo, or multi-acred estate. It's my earnest prayer that God is blessing your home with all things good and wonderful, and that the memories you're storing in your heart will be your touchstones of love for as long as you live.

A Friend...Touched by the Light

Someone gave me your book of paintings called *Home is Where the Heart is* as a gift. I just love it. Your paintings have touched my heart and soul. I admire you so much as an artist. When I look at your work, I am so touched that I almost feel like crying. God has graced you with a wonderful talent. Keep up the beautiful work. God bless you.

AMELIA HENDRICKS

The LORD your God in your midst,
The Mighty One, will save;
He will rejoice over you with gladness,
He will quiet you with His Love,
He will rejoice over you with singing.

ZEPHANIAH 3:17

TOUCHED BY THE
LIGHT OF GOD'S WORD

For the perverse person is an abomination

to the LORD,

But His secret counsel is with the upright.

The curse of the LORD is on the house

of the wicked,

But He blesses the home of the just.

Surely He scorns the scornful,

But gives grace to the humble.

PROVERBS 3:32–34

The LORD sat enthroned at the Flood,

And the LORD sits as King forever.

The LORD will give strength to His people;

The LORD will bless His people with peace.

PSALM 29:10–11

Touched by the Light of Experience

The fine edge of character had been blunted in the Rome of the second century A.D. The stern face of the traditional father of the family had faded out; instead we see on every hand the flabby face of the son of the house, the eternal spoiled child of society, who has grown accustomed to luxury and lost all sense of discipline . . . Some evaded the duty of maternity for fear of losing their looks. Some were not content to live their lives by their husband's side.

JEROME CARCOPINO

Be he a king
or a peasant,
he is happiest who
finds peace
at home.

JOHANN WOLFGANG
VON GOETHE

A Prayer to the Giver of Light

Father and Lord, thank You for giving us homes, be they remote, idyllic cottages surrounded by Your natural beauty or dwellings in crowded suburbs. Help us to remember that *home is where the heart is . . .* and that *the heart is where the home is.* While we face challenges in raising our children *Your way* and continue to address all manner of issues in our lives, we know You will stand near to us, O Giver of Light, spilling the blinding brilliance of Your holiness on to our paths. Help us to want more for our spouse, our friends and our children than we demand for ourselves. Remove our tired spirits from the clamor and diversion of television and needing to be continually online, and bring us together. Grant us the heart of a child, the wisdom of a maturing adult, and the spiritual discernment of one who strives to be conformed to image of Your Son, the Light of the world, the One who calls us from the scourge of darkness into the glory and majesty of Your marvelous light. Amen.

But every house where Love abides
And Friendship is a guest,
Is surely home, and
home–sweet–home;
For there the heart can rest.

HENRY VAN DYKE

In the spiritual realm,
as well as in the natural,
your return will be proportional
to your investment. *But this I say:*
He who sows sparingly will also
reap sparingly, and he who sows bountifully
will also reap bountifully.

(2 CORINTHIANS 9:6).

The earth is the LORD's, and all its fullness,
The world and those who dwell therein.
For He has founded it upon the seas,
And established it upon the waters.

PSALM 24:1-2

The Sea of Tranquility

It is the bent of the human spirit to seek on distant shores what ultimately can be found lodged deep in our hearts. It's the story of *diamonds in our own back yard* all over again. We often spend time, money, and energy—exhausting our bodies in the process—seeking peace, harmony, and tranquility *out there* some place. In fact, our own "sea of tranquility" is not a single place at all. It is all places, for it is buried within ourselves.

In this painting I've attempted to articulate the reality that life is a journey. For some, it's the same inner voyage repeated, or, perhaps, they've not yet left the harbor. For others, each day is an exciting visit to new horizons, challenging experiences, and fresh vistas. Wherever your voyage is taking you, you can travel in peace and tranquility at this moment if you will but allow the Light of the world, the person of Jesus Christ, to guide you.

In *The Sea of Tranquility* I found myself making love to the canvas as I moved from that first "block" of painting to the final dry brushing of the images—the lighthouse, the placid sea, and the illumined horizon. I felt emotion and passion intermingle a symbolism that speaks to the quiet harbor a merciful God has provided for his people. It is my prayer that your life may be a *sea of tranquility* in the midst of the storms and stress of modern-day living.

A Friend . . . Touched by the Light

I want to thank you for being such an inspiration. Almost three years

ago I became very ill. I developed one horrible disease after another,

but the doctors never could diagnose them properly. It was while I was

sitting in the doctor's office that I saw one of your paintings for the first

time. It moved my spirit, and its beauty caused me to contemplate my

life. I have always loved art, and in my youth it was dream to become

an artist. Seeing your work inspired me once again.

You have been my teacher, my mentor and, as time would prove, my

healer. Where the doctors failed, your inspirational work succeeded.

I believe with all my heart that God guides you, and I believe your

paintings have caused some of that to spill over on to me. Words

could never express what your paintings have brought to me—and

what you have brought to me. Thank you.

JANET AUBUCHON

TOUCHED BY THE
LIGHT OF GOD'S WORD

"The LORD make His face shine upon you,

And be gracious to you;

The LORD lift up His countenance upon you,

And give you peace."

NUMBERS 6:25–26

Open the gates,

That the righteous nation

which keeps the truth may enter in.

You will keep him in perfect peace,

Whose mind is stayed on You,

Because he trusts in You.

ISAIAH 26:2–3

Touched by the Light of Experience

Peace does not dwell in outward things, but within the soul;
we may preserve it in the midst of the bitterest pain, if our
will remain firm and submissive. Peace in this life springs
from submission, not in an exemption from suffering.

FENELON, ARCHBISHOP OF CAMBRAI, FRANCE

In life troubles will come which seem as if
they never will pass away. The night and the
storm look as though they will last forever;
but calm and the morning cannot be stayed;
the storm in its very nature is transient. The
effort of nature, as that of the human heart, is
to return to its repose, for God is peace.

GEORGE MACDONALD

A Prayer to the Giver of Light

Giver of light, make our hearts content to
lead a tranquil life. In that serenity may we
see the importance of obedience to Your
word and Your truth as we determine to
be willing daily to carry Your cross.
Open our hearts to a disciplined life
of peace even as the tempests blow mightily
about us. Grant us an inner strength that
only You can provide. May we draw on
Your power and be nourished only by You
and the life of Your Son, Jesus Christ. *Help*
us to remember that the outgoing tide invariably
welcomes the turn of the tide. Give us the
grace to discipline our temptations and
order our lives after Your expectations.
Dear Lord, just as You calmed the violent
seas with a simple *peace, be still,* may You
also calm our troubled souls, and lead us
gently into a sea of tranquility today, and
for all days to come. Amen.

Oh, love the LORD, all you His saints! For the LORD preserves the faithful.

PSALM 31:23

Bridge of Faith

Thomas Kinkade

Bridges. They're everywhere. There's the Brooklyn Bridge, the Golden Gate Bridge, the Howrah Bridge of Calcutta, India, and the Tsing Ma Bridge in Hong Kong . . . to name only a few of the tens of thousands of bridges throughout the world. There's also the "bridge over troubled waters," a song—and message—made famous by singers Paul Simon and Art Garfunkel, and a bridge we've all crossed more than we'd like to admit.

However, *bridges of the spirit* don't make the list of the world's great spans. Perhaps it's because they're seen neither as architectural marvels nor monuments to the genius of human engineering. Although my painting *Bridge of Faith* might never be included in an anthology of the bridges of the world, I consider myself every bit as much a bridge–builder as those who engineer massive structures of steel and concrete.

For me, to traverse the *Bridge of Faith* is to take one step closer to understanding God's goodness—a journey that's often messy and always unpredictable. As you look closely at this painting, you'll discover the bridge has withstood the test of time. It's no longer a perfect bridge. Travelers have worn away the stones, depriving the span of its once pristine quality. However, a well–traveled bridge has no choice but to reflect the ravages of time. And in its being worn, it shouts its usefulness, because a bridge has only one purpose: to take people over obstacles to where they want to go. For me, the *Bridge of Faith* has just enough dappled light to help take me take one more step on my way to the Eternal.

Where is your bridge of faith taking you? Is it in a joyful, tranquil direction? Is it moving you closer to your heavenly Father and to all He promises to his children? As a fellow traveler on the road to discovery, I would sincerely like to know.

A Friend... Touched by the Light

Having *Stairway to Paradise* in our family room reminds us of how our baby must have left our home and traveled up to heaven. And it is so beautiful!

We find solace in thinking of our baby, where he or she will never feel pain or have the sinful nature that those of us in this world have to deal with. I can easily see our child in a beautiful place, not unlike your paintings—laughing and playing. While you obviously didn't paint that picture for us, it certainly was God's hand that lead us to it. I hope you continue to touch other people's hearts in the same way you've touched us.

TONY AND ANGELA ARES

TOUCHED BY THE LIGHT
OF GOD'S WORD

"For the vision is yet for an appointed time;

But at the end it will speak, and it will not lie.

Though it tarries, wait for it;

Because it will surely come,

It will not tarry.

Behold the proud,

His soul is not upright in him;

But the just shall live by his faith."

HABAKKUK 2:3–4

And those who sat at the table with Him began to say to
themselves, "Who is this who even forgives sins?" Then He
said to the woman, "Your faith has saved you. Go in peace."

LUKE 7:49–50

Touched by the Light of Experience

Faith and obedience are bound up in the same bundle;
he that obeys God, trusts God;
and he that trusts God, obeys God.
He that is without faith is without works,
and he that is without works is without faith.

CHARLES HADDON SPURGEON

Faith makes the uplook good,
the outlook bright,
and the future glorious.

A Prayer to the Giver of Light

Dear heavenly Father, thank You for the bridges You provide for our daily living: bridges of love, hope and faith—for without them, how could we possibly get to the other side of our fears and discouragements? Even as You provide these bridges that span the deep chasms of our uncertainties and tears, may You continue to give us the resources to build bridges of our own— bridges that lead people to love You, trust You, honor You, and to consider receiving the life–preserving message of Your Son Jesus Christ.

When our hopes are dashed,
keep leading us to that bridge of faith.
When our best–laid plans fail,
keep pointing us to that bridge of faith.
When we have nowhere else to turn,
keep your divine pools of light on that
bridge of faith so we will not lose our way.
Amen.

Oh, that men would give thanks to the LORD for His goodness, And for His wonderful works to the children of me

PSALM 107:8

Victorian Christmas

Thomas Kinkade

Making yourself a home is a matter of creating a place of quiet rest for your weary heart. This is what I hope I've accomplished in *Victorian Christmas*, the painting of a stately old home that stands on a prominent street corner in my hometown, Placerville, California. It was my intention to turn back the clock to a Christmas Eve celebration around the turn of the century and paint this magnificent residence lit up for holiday festivities.

Based on the response I've received from this painting, I sense I've struck a nerve in the spirits of many who long for a reprieve from the chaos of modern living. Yes, the people walking in the painting undoubtedly have their shares of problems. The children on their sleds probably are not perfect children. The man bringing the gift to the front door might not be the ideal husband. But at least the scene is not replete with boys and girls listening mindlessly to rock music on headphones or people arguing. You'll also not see—or *hear*—a boom box–outfitted, smog–producing vehicle polluting the atmosphere. One thing we can assume: *the man driving the carriage probably never got stopped for speeding.*

As the light of day ebbs into a rich, northern California sunset, I urge you to place yourself in this picture. As you do, I hope you feel the sheer over–the–top joy of the community that exists between children, animals, and adults alike. Let your eye be drawn into each segment of the painting, and let every one of them speak to you. Although you might not have the privilege of living in such a world of snowy beauty, it is more than possible to ask the original Painter of light, God Himself, to grant you the kind of peace, joy, and love that can make every day a *Victorian Christmas* in your heart. And that is all that really matters.

From the bottom of my heart

Thank you.

1 Mr. Kinkade,

A Friend . . . Touched by the Light

Thank you for sharing your gift with the world. This gives

us the opportunity just to sit down and reflect on what

the future holds for the righteous ones (Psalm 37:29).

What keeps us going day after day, when we lose a loved

one are *memories*, and the visual stimulation of beautiful

things that reach the core of our hearts. May God continue

to bless your hands with every stroke of the painter's brush.

CANDEE MARIE RAMOS

TOUCHED BY THE LIGHT
OF GOD'S WORD

. . . that we should no longer be children, tossed to and fro and carried about with every wind of doctrine, by the trickery of men, in the cunning craftiness of deceitful plotting, but, speaking the truth in love, may grow up in all things into Him who is the head—Christ—from whom the whole body, joined and knit together by what every joint supplies, according to the effective working by which every part does its share, causes growth of the body for the edifying of itself in love.

EPHESIANS 4:14–16

. . . Become complete. Be of good comfort,
be of one mind, live in peace; and the God
of love and peace will be with you.

2 CORINTHIANS 13:11

Touched by the Light of Experience

Sun of my soul! Thou Savior dear,

It is not night if Thou be near.

JOHN KEBLE

God still speaks
His voice of love to those
who take the time to listen.
Where love is,
there is God also.

LEO TOLSTOY

A Prayer to the Giver of Light

Father and Giver of light, we thank You for helping us see our life as You meant us to live it. Although we cannot all enjoy living in the splendor of a Victorian mansion and take pleasure in the idyllic atmosphere of a snowy Christmas Eve, You make it possible for us to possess a heart of joy that is every bit as meaningful. You paint the light of hope in our weary hearts. *Thank You.* Your divine brushstrokes crisscross our spirits and enable us to love others and ourselves. *Thank You.* Most wonderful of all, You've given us Your Son, the Light of the world, who casts great beams of light on our path so we will neither stumble nor fall. *Thank You. Thank You, from the bottom of our hearts.*

Now may the God of hope fill you

with all joy and peace in believing,

that you may abound in hope

by the power of the Holy Spirit.

ROMANS 15:13

The Garden of Prayer

As I sat before my easel to paint *The Garden of Prayer*, I asked God to guide my brushstrokes into a singular act of worship. The natural beauty of God's world touches me so deeply that I have no choice but to capture its splendor on canvas. But it's so much more than putting dabs of paint on little pieces of cloth; more than mathematically lining up images so that each is in perspective; it's more than putting glaze upon glaze so that portions can be removed to allow the light finally to shine through in a radiance all its own.

While all that activity took place to produce the painting, my deeper purpose was to create a *Garden of Prayer*, where I might come to celebrate my love for God, and to invite my friends to enter and enjoy our Father's bounty with me. Although I am the painter, it is almighty God who gives us the rock–strewn stream, the flowers of many hues, the carpet of grass with its dappled light, and munificence of a lighted sky that *only* He can create.

As you enter this garden with me, let us approach His presence in silence. May our hearts be one with the psalmist who wisely wrote, *Be still and know that I am God* (Psalm 46:10). May the pools of our experience, as in the painting, become deeper than the next, demonstrating that we are growing in the things that truly matter. Just as Jesus went to His own quiet place, let us also approach our own *garden of prayer* in a spirit of worship and love.

A Friend . . . Touched by the Light

I am a kindergarten teacher for a Cincinnati public school, and I own a version of *The Garden of Prayer*. During my art history class I was able to bring in a blown–up picture of my painting. The students would not let me move on! They kept coming back. I was able to get them all post cards, and ten of the thirteen students would not take them home for fear of their parents or siblings taking them. So I allowed them to keep the post cards on their desks all year. Every time the students wanted "alone time," they would go to their desks and enjoy them—or just to get their feelings out. Not only has *The Garden of Prayer* created a special bond between my mother and me, but it's also a sanctuary for my five and six year-olds. Thank you for touching our hearts and for giving them hope for the future.

SHAWN OLIVIA PHILLIPS

TOUCHED BY THE LIGHT OF GOD'S WORD

"Thus it was beautiful in greatness and in the
length of its branches,

Because its roots reached to abundant waters.

The cedars in the garden of God could not hide it;

The fir trees were not like its boughs,

And the chestnut trees were not like its branches;

No tree in the garden of God was like it in beauty.

I made it beautiful with a multitude of branches,

So that all the trees of Eden envied it,

That were in the garden of God."

EZEKIEL 31:7–9

Let your gentleness be known to all men.
The Lord is at hand. Be anxious for nothing, but in
everything by prayer and supplication, with thanksgiving,
let your requests be made known to God; and the peace
of God, which surpasses all understanding, will guard
your hearts and minds through Christ Jesus.

PHILIPPIANS 4:5–7

Touched by the Light of Experience

*To be a Christian without prayer is no more possible
than to be alive without breathing.*

MARTIN LUTHER

*My heart is awed
within me when I think
Of the great miracle that still goes on,
In silence, round me—
the perpetual work
Of Thy creation, finished,
yet renewed forever.
Written on Thy works I read
The less of Thy own eternity.*

WILLIAM CULLEN BRYANT

More things
are wrought by prayer
than this world dreams of.

ALFRED, LORD TENNYSON

A Prayer to the Giver of Light

Loving God, You are the only true Painter of light. We worship you and bathe ourselves in the beauty of Your handiwork. Take us often to the garden of prayer where we may enlarge our thoughts of You, see You for who You truly are, and where we can allow You to keep shaping us into the people You designed us to be. We stand in awe before this universe You created for our pleasure. We kneel in reverence before You, O God, grateful for how You reveal Yourself in splashes and shades of color, pools of water, and sunrises and sunsets that only Your divine brushstrokes can create. We now enter our garden of prayer. Make us worthy of being in Your presence today and for every day to come. Thank You for being our Painter of light. Amen.

Light and Beauty
are all around us.

They intensify moments of joy, bubble amid the merry din of holidays, and soothe us during times of grief or uncertainty.

The Lord of Light blesses us with glimpses of the eternal. The Creator has left His fingerprints all over this world. Artists—in fact, all lovers of beauty—try to capture those eternal moments through words, paper, canvas, clay, computer, or even merely in memory. When we see the light of God, we know it, and we treasure it.

But light isn't just what we see—it's what we are called to be.

Jesus said to the believers, "You are the light of the world" (Matthew 5:14). And Paul wrote that light should characterize our lives: "Do all things without complaining and disputing, that you may become blameless and harmless, children of God without fault in the midst of a crooked and perverse generation, among whom you shine as lights in the world, holding fast the word of life" (Philippians 2:14-16).

When you find beauty in this world, know that it is merely a poor reflection of the glory that is to come. May you find the light in every day. May you be light to all whom you encounter. And may you live forever in God's pure, holy radiance.

Arise, shine, for your light has come! and the glory of the
LORD is risen upon you.

ISAIAH 60:1

Author's Note

Many thanks to the thousands of friends whose letters have inspired me over the years. I am humbled that my work has touched your lives. The letters included in this book are just a handful of the kind notes I've received—thank you for allowing me to share your words.

I pray that each of you will continue to share the Source of all light, and to encourage each other as you have encouraged me.

The city had no need of the sun or

of the moon to shine in it,

for the glory of God illuminated it.

The Lamb is its light.

And the nations of those

who are saved shall walk in its light,

and the kings of the earth

bring their glory and honor into it.

REVELATION 21:23-23